Rhyme Me a Rhyme

by Jane Belk Moncure

illustrated by Marc Belenchia

THE CHILD'S WORLD

ELGIN, ILLINOIS 60120

Library of Congress Cataloging in Publication Data

Moncure, Jane Belk
Rhyme me a rhyme.

SUMMARY: In bed with a sore throat, Goat is cheered by her animal friends who bring her gifts with rhymes.
[1. Stories in rhyme. 2. Animals—Fiction]
I. Belenchia, Marc. II. Title.
PZ8.3.M72Rh [E] 76-16538
ISBN 0-913778-42-7

Distributed by Childrens Press, 1224 West Van Buren Street, Chicago, Illinois 60607

One morning in May, a sweet little goat
went sailing away in her own little boat.

But the boat did not float.

The goat lost her coat.

Poor goat developed a very sore throat.
"You must stay in bed!"
the goat doctor said.

So her friends came to visit her, one at a time.
To cheer her up, each one brought her a rhyme.
The fox brought her something in a box.

"Is this a tie

or two pairs of socks?"
asked the fox.

Goat answered, "Socks!
Thank you, Fox."

The cat brought her something in a hat.

"Is it a bird,

or a ball and a bat?"
asked the cat.

"A ball and a bat in a hat!"
said the goat. "Thank you, Cat."

Five butterflies brought a small surprise.
"Close your eyes," said the butterflies.

"Is this a book

or a strawberry pie?"
asked a butterfly.

(What do you think the good goat said?
Make a guess. Figure it out in your head.)

Two kangaroos jumped up the stairs.
"We brought you things that come in pairs.

“Two pairs of gloves

or two pairs of shoes?”
asked the kangaroos.

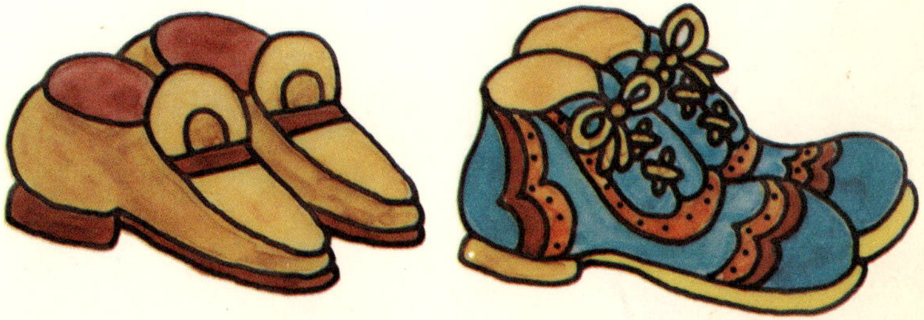

(What is the answer, gloves or shoes?
Which was the gift of the kangaroos?)

The ape brought a package to the goat.
"Here's something to wear when you sail in your boat.

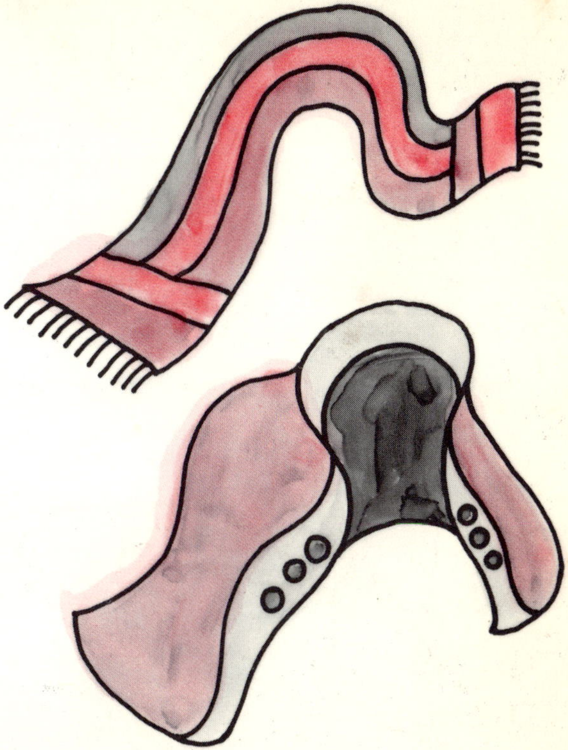

Is it a scarf

or a lovely cape?"
asked the ape.

(You know.
Isn't that so?)

Brown Bear also gave her something to wear.

"Is it a dress

or a bow for your hair?"
asked Bear.

Bunny gave goat something funny.

"Is this a balloon

or a bank full of money?"
asked Bunny.

"Great!" said the goat.
"I can buy a new boat."
She quickly got over
her bad sore throat.

She bought a new boat,
one that would float.

She wrote each friend a little note.

"Thank you for rhyming me a rhyme.
Come sailing with me anytime!"

When she sailed with the fox,
she wore her ______.   socks

When she sailed with the cat,
she wore her ____   hat
and took her ______________.   ball and bat

When she sailed with the kangaroos,
she wore her ______.   shoes

When she sailed with the ape,
she wore her _____.   cape

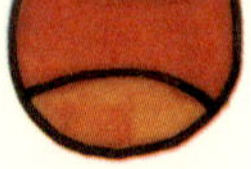
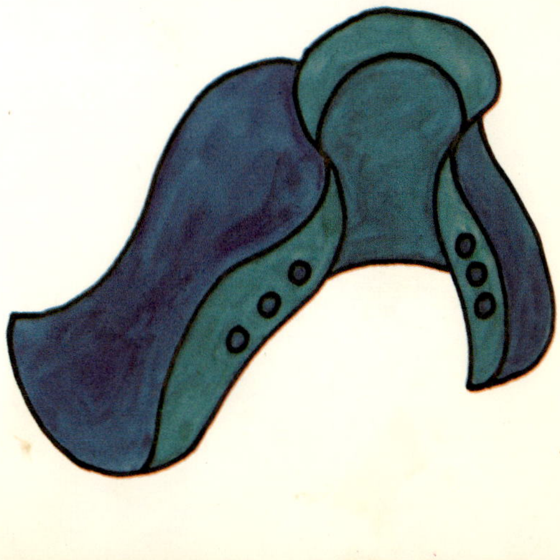

When she sailed with the bear,
she wore a bow in her _____. hair

When she sailed with butterflies,
she made more strawberry _____. pies

Then the goat had a wonderful new idea.

“If my friends will rhyme me another rhyme,
I will have a party, anytime!”

So the goat gave a party. My, what a treat!

Guess what! There is one empty seat.

The seat is for you.
Goat says, "Rhyme me a rhyme.
Join my party anytime!"